12/26/91

To: Arianne

Merry Christmas!

Love,

Mom & Dad

The
Other
Side
of the
Door

Also by Jeff Moss
With Illustrations by Chris Demarest

THE BUTTERFLY JAR

The Other Side of the Door

Poems by *Jeff Moss*

Illustrated by *Chris Demarest*

BANTAM BOOKS

NEW YORK TORONTO LONDON

SYDNEY AUCKLAND

THE OTHER SIDE OF THE DOOR
A Bantam Book / November 1991

Library of Congress Cataloging-in-Publication Data:

Moss, Jeffrey.
   The other side of the door : poems / by Jeff Moss : illustrated by
Chris Demarest
      p.   cm.
   Includes index.
   Summary: A collection of humorous and fanciful poetry about a
variety of situations both real and imaginary.
   ISBN 0-553-07259-5
   [1. American poetry. 2. Humorous poetry.] I. Demarest, Chris
L., ill. II. Title.
PS3563.088458084   1991
811'.54—dc20   91-10441
                                                                    CIP
                                                                    AC

Published simultaneously in the United States and Canada

Bantam Books are published by Bantam Books, a division of Bantam Double-
day Dell Publishing Group, Inc. Its trademark, consisting of the words "Bantam
Books" and the portrayal of a rooster, is Registered in U.S. Patent and Trade-
mark Office and in other countries. Marca Registrada. Bantam Books, 666 Fifth
Avenue, New York, New York 10103.

PRINTED IN THE UNITED STATES OF AMERICA

RRH   0   9   8   7   6   5   4   3   2   1

In Memory of Jim Henson

and

To Welcome A.B.J.M.

The
Other
Side
of the
Door

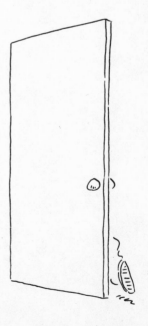

The Other Side Of The Door

On the other side of the door
I can be a different me,
As smart and as brave and as funny or strong
As a person could want to be.
There's nothing too hard for me to do,
There's no place I can't explore
Because everything can happen
On the other side of the door.

On the other side of the door
I don't have to go alone.
If you come, too, we can sail tall ships
And fly where the wind has flown.
And wherever we go, it is almost sure
We'll find what we're looking for
Because everything can happen
On the other side of the door.

The Splinter

Eliot Eggleston had a splinter
That wouldn't come out until next winter.
His mom got a tweezer and tried to squeeze it
But the splinter was too big for a tweezer to tweeze it.
So they called in a handyman named Clarence McNab
But the splinter was too big for his pliers to grab.
Last came the Splinter Squad with sirens and gongs
And they finally got the splinter out with fireplace tongs.
Eliot's splinter—imagine that!
(He uses it today as a baseball bat.)

If The Sea Were Over The Sky

If the sea were over the sky
Would minnows and motorboats fly?
Would each eagle you met
Be all soaking wet?
And would seals and eels always be dry?

The Bug In The Bathroom Sink

There's a big yucchy bug in the bathroom sink,
I could turn on the water and drown it, I think.
Or else I could squash it, I'd get all prepared
With a rolled-up newspaper, I'm not at all scared
Of that great big yucchy nasty thing,
Though I certainly hope he's not the kind that can sting.
No, I'm not at all nervous when I hear him buzz
(Except my heart is beating faster than it usually does.)
I'll just get some bug spray and off he'll fly.
I'll get rid of that bug just as easy as pie.
It'll be so simple, there'll be nothing to it!
Except since you're older . . . I'll let you do it.

Bill

I'm giving away my old doll, Bill,
I told Mom it's all right.
I'm too old now for a doll like Bill,
I sleep by myself at night.
But when I was little and when I got sad,
He was always there to play.
So maybe I'll ask Mom to keep him for me,
For when I have a kid someday.

I Think I'm Going To Sneeze Soon

I think I'm going to sneeze soon,
I'm just not quite sure when.
I've got that tickle in my nose
And . . . Ooops! . . . WHOOPS! . . . (No, not then.)
My handkerchief is ready,
It'll feel so good when I do.
But I guess it's not going to happen now,
So I might as well . . .

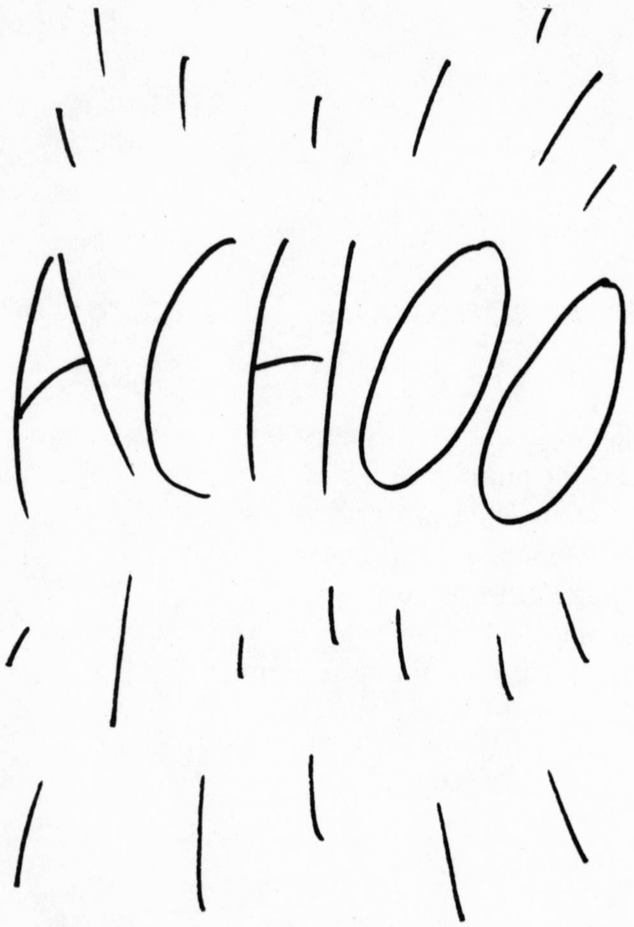
ACHOO

Things You Can Do While You're Talking On The Phone

You can stand on your head.
You can wiggle your toes.
You can make a face.
You can twiddle your nose.
You can cross your eyes.
You can scratch your knees.
('Cause the person on the other end
Never sees!)

The Skorse

An amazing animal is the skorse.
He's partly skunk and he's partly horse.
And when he leaves an unpleasant aroma,
He just holds his nose and gallops on home-a.

What To Tell Your Parents When They Say, "Well, If You're Too Full To Eat That Broccoli, I Guess You're Too Full To Eat Dessert"

Tell them: Everyone's stomach is divided into compartments for different foods. Here is a drawing of mine.

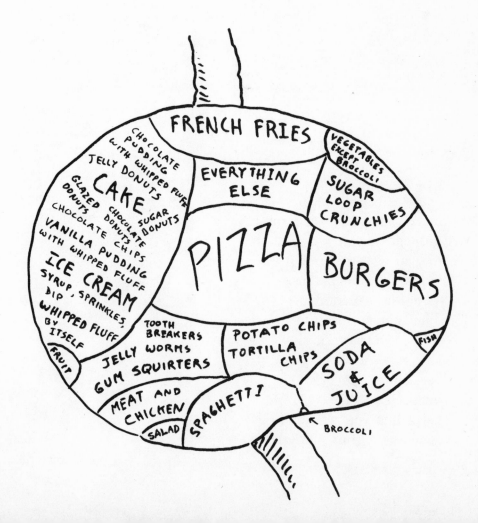

I'm Glad That I'm Not Famous

I'm glad that I'm not famous,
I'm glad I'm not a star.
I'm glad I'm not known everywhere
Like famous people are.
When you're famous, they all whisper
When they see you on the street,
And in the cafeteria
They bug you when you eat.
Everywhere you travel,
You stick out like a giraffe.
Even when you're shopping,
People want your autograph.

They make you sign your name
For all their nephews and their nieces
And then they need to shake your hand
And pinch your cheek to pieces.
And then they follow you on tour
And almost cause a riot,
You never get your privacy
And never any quiet.
They ask you for your shoelaces
As souvenirs to keep
And wait all night outside your house
So you can never sleep.

So I'm glad that I'm not famous
'Cause I never would survive.
I just wish that Cathy Delafield . . .
Knew I was alive.

Does The Sky Begin?

Does the sky begin at the top of my head
Or does it begin up higher?
Does it begin at the roof of our house
Or above the telephone wire?
Does it begin just below the clouds
Or above the trees so tall?
Or is it just that the sky begins
And no one knows where at all?

The Clam

I ate my first clam ever
Just a minute or two ago.
My cousin Michael dared me
So how could I say no?
It looked the most disgusting
So I gulped it in a daze.
That clam is in my stomach now
(And I sure hope it stays).

Stuart McGroo

Let me tell you the story of Stuart McGroo,
A person who never tried anything new.
As a boy he ate nothing but gooseberry pie,
Not one bit of any new food would he try,
Not one pea or donut, not one brussels sprout,
And that's what young Stuart McGroo was about.

He would make no new friends so you couldn't invite
Stuart over to your house to stay for the night.
"I like my own bed!" cried young Stuart McGroo.
"I'm a person who never tries anything new!
I will stay safe at home! I will never go out!"
And that's what young Stuart McGroo was about.

Well, Stuart grew up but his heart did not throb
To raise a nice family or have a good job.
He just stayed in bed with his gooseberry pie
Saying, "Families and jobs are just new things to try
And I *never* try new things, there can be no doubt!"
And that is what Stuart McGroo was about.

The years hurried by, Stuart grew old alone
But he wondered about things that he'd never known.
And one day an old man with beard and a cane
Was seen strolling slowly down Tea Garden Lane.
He smiled at the people, they smiled at him, too,
And he made some new friends, did old Stuart McGroo.

Then a family he met asked him home for a meal.
For the first time he tasted spaghetti and veal
And pudding and milk and he loved every bite.
And Stuart dreamed happy dreams all through that night
Till he woke with a start and let out a shout,
"Now I finally see what the world's all about!"

Another Day

Last Friday I hated my teacher
And Linda and Peter and Jill
And Mandy and Greg and my mother,
The mailman and Sandy and Phil.
But today something's changed and I like them,
Who knows what that something could be?
It must be today they're all different.
(I'm sure that it couldn't be me.)

Walls

Walls are quite useful,
Here is what they're for:
Walls keep your ceiling
From falling on your floor.

Amanda

Amanda happens to be the best athlete in our school.
   She wins every gymnastics meet. She beat Peter
   Montoya in a race. She is the second baseman on our
   baseball team. (Some kids say she is the second
   base*person*, which is, I guess, correct.)

Amanda is also pretty smart and kind of cool looking.
   She's the kind of person that when she does
   something great, she usually just says "Nice going"
   to everybody else on the team, so almost nobody doesn't
   like her.

There are a few kids who probably wish her name was Ted
   or Ralph or something, but the best thing is that
   most of us are proud of Amanda and we think she's
   a really good guy. (Some kids say she is a really
   good *person*, which is, I guess, correct.)

Katie Brown's Mother

Katie Brown's mother is not a good cook,
Her scrambled eggs taste just like glue.
Her spaghetti resembles wet pieces of straw,
Her hamburgers taste like a shoe.
But nevertheless we will always say yes
When Katie invites us to dinner,
'Cause her mother and Kate are both really great
And at least it's a way to get thinner.

The Haircut

I knew I should have stopped him
  just as soon as he began it.
That barber left me looking
  like the beast from some lost planet.
It's like he used a lawn mower
  and then my hair got sat on.
Oh well, I'll just go through the next six years
  with this dumb hat on.

Breakfast

I C U 8 your scrambled X,
I C U drank your T.
My heart is filled with NV,
R there NE X 4 me?
O Y is the carton MT now?
How greedy can U B?
4 U 8 all the scrambled X
And left me 1 green P!

What I Explained To Mom When She Said That Leah Is More Polite Than I Am

I said,
"Leah is very polite
When she stays with us overnight.
But when I stay over at Leah's
I'm even polit-er than she is."
So Mom said, "Please, when I see ya,
Pretend that you're visiting Leah."

Foot Ball

A royal ball is a party
Where princes and princesses meet,
So it must be true that a foot ball
Is a party for lots of feet.

The McSloppys

"I have just learned of something that they call soap!"
Cried Mrs. Cornelia McSloppy.
"Such a terrible thing, it could make you lose hope!"
Cried Mrs. Cornelia McSloppy.
"I saw it right here in this magazine!
It's all squooshy and slippery and sudsy and green!
It's a horrible thing that could make us all clean!"
Cried Mrs. Cornelia McSloppy.

"I have just heard of something that's called a drawer!"
Cried Mr. Alphonso McSloppy.
"So awful I don't want to hear any more!"
Cried Mr. Alphonso McSloppy.
"We drop clothes on the floor and leave them there!
But drawers hold your socks and your underwear!
They could make our rooms neat! It just isn't fair!"
Cried Mr. Alphonso McSloppy.

"I saw something called napkins on my TV!"
Cried little Cecilia McSloppy.
"They are horrible things, you can take it from me!"
Cried little Cecilia McSloppy.
"Napkins won't let you drip jam on your shirt!
They keep you from smearing your lap with dessert!
Beware of all napkins! They'll keep off the dirt!"
Cried little Cecilia McSloppy.

Now aren't *you* glad that your room is so neat?
(And not like the family McSloppy?)
Don't you love keeping clean from your hair to your feet?
(Not at all like the family McSloppy.)
You never spill food on your shirt or your dress.
Just the thought of un-neatness would cause you distress.
'Cause it wouldn't be fun to be making a mess
Like that silly old family McSloppy!

(Or would it? . . .)

Warren

Warren always tells us
How he's *best* or *first* or *most*.
He boasts about his bike, his street,
His clothes, his house, his toast!
It seems like everything he has
Is always *best* or *first*.
But the funny thing about Warren is
We all think he's the *worst*.

A New Pair Of Shoes

If a visitor from Mars saw a new pair of shoes,
She'd say, "How strange that they come in twos!
I'll put them right on and I'll tie them up neat,
Too bad I'll have to walk around with seven bare feet!"

April

So far
In April
I . . .

Lost my pencils,
Cut my knee,
Missed the school bus,
Got a D,
Fought with Martha,
Yelled at Gail,
Ripped my sweater
On a nail,
Dropped my lunch plate,
Lost my key,
Didn't win
The spelling bee,
Baked a cake
And made a mess,
Broke my bike,
Stained my dress,
And learned that Meg
Is moving away . . .
So on this rainy
April day,
There's only one thing
Left to say:
I'm very glad
It's almost May.

Why I'm Glad I'm Not A Worm

I'd feel so blue
When people went, "Eeeyuuuuu!"

What Not To Give A Beetlebug

Don't ever give a beetlebug
A bowling-ball gift,
'Cause a bowling ball's too heavy
For a beetlebug to lift.

He can't fit it in his doorway,
He can't keep it in his hall,
His garage won't even hold it
'Cause the ceiling's not that tall,
And although he might appreciate
A gift that's very small,
Like a jellybean or pebble,
He won't like a bowling ball
Because if it started rolling,
It might crash right through his wall.
It might break his lamps and dishes
And his chandelier might fall.
It might bonk him on his beetle head
And send him in a sprawl.
Yes, a bowling ball is something
Beetlebugs can't use at all!

So don't ever give a beetlebug
A bowling ball present,
'Cause a disappointed beetlebug
Is something quite unpleasant.

Bernard

If Bernard was the only name in the world . . .
Then the man who discovered America would be
    Bernard Columbus
And the first President of the United States would be
    Bernard Washington.
You'd sing nursery rhymes like, "Bernard Had a Little Lamb"
And read fairy tales like "Bernard and the Seven Dwarfs."
When you introduced a friend of yours to another friend of
    yours, you'd say, "Bernard, I'd like you to meet Bernard."
Sometimes you might even say, "Bernard, I'd like you to meet
    my sister, Bernard."
It's certainly a good thing there are other names.

A Poem To Turn Upside Down
(If You Want To Finish Reading It)

I
really
love
my

MOM

and
how!
Because
my
mom
is
really . . .

Stubbed Toe

I hate it when I stub my toe,
I want to know how come
A thing that brings me so much pain
Can make me feel so dumb.

Best Friends

Kristy says she has a best friend,
And a best best friend,
But she says I'm her best best best friend.
I told her I think people should have just one best friend with
    one "best."
Otherwise you could have a best best best best best best best
    best best best best best friend
And whoever was just your best best best friend would think
    you probably didn't like them very much at all.

In Bed With A Bad Cold

I've got to blow by doze!
I've got to blow by doze!
By doze is stuffed and I feel so sick
I'll call by Bobby and she'll cub quick
With a bunch of tissues soft and thick
'Cause I've got to blow by doze!

Babies

That tough western cowboy out herding his cattle
Once lay in his crib with a blankie and rattle.
The TV news lady, though this may seem strange,
Once sat in her diapers and needed a change.
Each major-league ball player once was so small
The one way to get to first base was to crawl,
And even your teacher who's so smart at school
Would lie in her playpen and gurgle and drool.
So love your new sister and please don't forget
Even *you* were once tiny and noisy and wet.

Madeleine Grauer

"I've got an earache!" said Madeleine Grauer.
"It's bad when it starts and gets worse by the hour!
It stings in my ear and it zings in my head
And that's why I'm crying!"
  young Madeleine said.

When her family moved to a home far away,
Her new classmates teased her and said, "You can't play!"
So alone in the girls' room she sat down and cried
And when kids wandered in, there was no place to hide.

So,
"I've got an earache!" said Madeleine Grauer.
"A serious ouch with a lot of pain-power!
It pings in my ear and it pongs in my head,
And that's why I'm crying!" young Madeleine said.

When Madeleine's faithful dog Max ran away,
Madeleine's heart felt all soggy and gray.
She sat in her yard and alone there she cried
But some kids passing by saw her all teary-eyed.

So,
"I've got an earache!" said Madeleine Grauer.
"It stings and it dings and it makes me feel sour!
It bonks in my ear and it zonks in my head
And that's why I'm crying!" young Madeleine said.

Well, Max wandered home after days had gone by.
Madeleine was so happy she started to cry.
The kids said, "An earache again! What a shame!"
But this time her answer was far from the same.

"No,
I don't have an earache!" said Madeleine Grauer.
"My heart feels as big as a blossoming flower.
I never had earaches or zonks in my head.
My feelings inside me were hurting instead.
Good ones or bad ones, your feelings can spread,
And sometimes they cause all the tears that you shed,
But now I'm as happy as a bear who's been fed—
And *that's* why I'm crying!" young Madeleine said.

What I'll Do To Make You Laugh

I'll ho-ho-ho and I'll chuck-chuck-chuckle.
I'll tee-hee-hee and I'll yuck-yuck-yuckle.
I'll hardy-har-har, and when I'm through,
If you're not laughing, I'll boo-hoo-hoo!

A Baby Rhinoceros

A baby rhinoceros sat on my knee,
That's not where I wanted that rhino to be.
A young hippopotamus stood on my toe,
That's not where I wanted that hippo to go.
A very small elephant lay on my foot,
That's not where I wanted that elephant put.
So I sent the three of them off to the zoo
Now they're very happy and . . .
My knee, toe, and foot are happy, too.

A Rhyme

I'm
Trying to make a rhyme
About the time
I found a dime.
But it's too hard to do it.
I knew it.

Maynard's Cousin

As bald as a melon was Maynard's cousin,
Still he was as happy as a honeybee buzzin'
'Cause Maynard's cousin had brains by the dozen
Down underneath where all his hair wuzzen.

I'm Going To Say I'm Sorry

I'm going to say I'm sorry.
It's time for this quarrel to end.
I know that we both didn't mean it
And each of us misses a friend.
It isn't much fun being angry
And arguing's just the worst,
So I'm going to say I'm sorry . . .
Just as soon as you say it first!

The Best Test

Make a check ☑ in one box only after each question.

1) What would you like to do best?

    a) go to a movie
    b) go to a ball game
    c) play with me at my house

        a) ☐ b) ☐ c) ☐

2) What would you like to be when you grow up?

    a) a marine biologist
    b) a teacher
    c) my friend

        a) ☐ b) ☐ c) ☐

3) What would you like to have best?

    a) a million dollars
    b) your own jet plane
    c) the clay pencil holder I made at school

        a) ☐ b) ☐ c) ☐

(If you checked c) ☑ every time, you can definitely be my friend but you are probably not too smart.)

Stegosaurus

If I had a stegosaurus for a pet, I would name him Reggie.
I would go outside and play with him whenever my mom was
    feeling edgy.
I'd walk him through the neighborhood on a leash (because
    otherwise it's against the law).
And I'd teach him to sit, lie down, and roll over, and to give me
    his claw.
Sometimes my dad and I would give him a bath
    while we were washing the car.

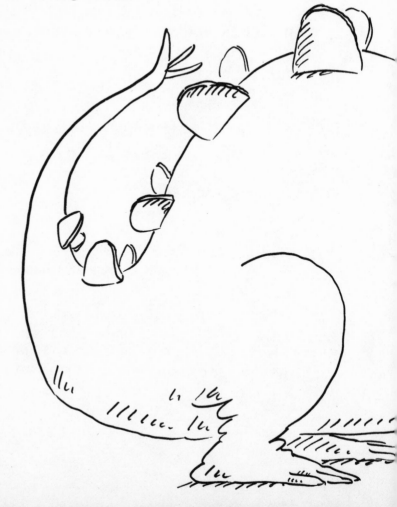

We'd need the large hose and the scrub brush with the long
 handle because that's how big stegosauruses are.
Then, at my sister's birthday party, she'd invite over all the little
 tykes,
And they'd go for steggy-back rides, making sure they held on
 tight to Reggie's spikes.
But best of all, at dinnertime, all the stuff I don't like—carrots,
 cabbage, spinach, etc.—would
 immediately become Reggie's,
Because stegosauruses are
 vegetarians (which, I'm sure
 you know, means that the only
 thing they ever eat is . . . veggies!)

Nursery Rhymes

Jack fell down and broke his crown
And didn't feel too well.
In "Rockabye Baby," the treetop broke
And the cradle and baby fell.
Poor Humpty Dumpty cracked to bits
When he tumbled off his wall.
(And the people who make up nursery rhymes
Must like to see people fall.)

Jeanie

My friend Jeanie has freckles on her nose
Special Jeanie freckles on her nose.
Some are bigger and some are teeny
But no one has freckles exactly like Jeanie.

My friend Jeanie is feeling mad today
Special Jeanie feeling mad today.
She looks like a dragon, she growls like a meanie
No one gets angry exactly like Jeanie.

My friend Jeanie has a goofy kind of laugh
A special Jeanie goofy kind of laugh.
But of all the people that I've ever seen-ie
Laughing or angry or happy or meanie
With freckles (some bigger and some of them teeny)
There's nobody nowhere exactly like Jeanie.

Pictures Of Grampa

Last Christmastime my Grampa Don died.
Grandma was saddest and even Dad cried.
Then the next week we visited Grandma and found
She'd put pictures of Grampa all around.
She'd put one in the kitchen, and one in the hall,
On the big special desk, and the living-room wall.
Almost wherever I looked I could see
Pictures of Grampa looking at me.

Grandma explained why she'd put them there—
When she missed Grampa most, she'd just sit in a chair
And look at the pictures, all on her own.
They made her feel not so much alone.
She could talk to them sometimes, when she passed one she
   might
Say, "Hello, Grampa Don" or "Dear Don, good night."
I know what she meant, I still talk to my bear
When it's late at night and there's no one there.

It's summer now and time has gone by.
We saw Grandma last week for the Fourth of July
And I looked for the pictures of Grampa Don
But they weren't there, they were all of them gone
Except for the one next to Grandma's bed
Where Grampa Don's smiling, with a tilt to his head.
I asked Grandma what she'd done with the rest.
She'd put them away, she thought that was best.

She told me she'd always miss Grampa Don
But he wasn't here and she had to go on.
Then she got out some cards and we played a game
And it seemed like things were just the same—
We both of us laughed and we both had fun,
We played Crazy Eights and Grandma won.
And then as she hugged me, I don't know why,
Grandma was happy, but she started to cry.

Faces

There are millions of kids in the world, all with two eyes, one
  nose, and a mouth
And of all those millions of faces, no two are exactly alike.
You'd think that by now there'd be no way left to put together
  eyes and noses and mouths to make faces that are different
  from every other face
But what's amazing is that there will keep on being millions and
  millions of different ways forever
And no two faces will ever be exactly the same.

Bad Mood

I am not in the mood for a hug.
I would rather get stung by a bug.
Please don't write, please don't phone,
Please just leave me alone
In this big deep dark hole that I've dug.

What To Say To A Tightrope Walker
With A Sore Throat

You better not cough
Or you might fall off.

The Twelve-Nosed Gazunk

The marvelous twelve-nosed gazunk
Is as lovely as you might have thunk.
She adores sniffing roses
But, having twelve noses,
She's glad that you
    aren't a skunk.

Pizza-Mouth

Did you ever have a piece of too-hot pizza
When the cheese was still all bubbly,
And you took a big bite and what happened next
Was something very troub-ly?
Like . . .
"Oooh! Ow! My mouth is on fire!
Woo! Yow! The flames are growing higher!
It's too hot to swallow! My teeth won't chew!
My tongue can't juggle it! . . . Ouch!! Oh!! Oooh!!
Bring snow or ice or anything cool!
Please throw my mouth in a swimming pool!
Ah . . . A glass of cold water . . . Oooh . . . Thanks a lot.
I never bit anything half so hot.
I'm sure even after this pain disappears
The roof of my mouth will be shredded for years."

And whether you come from the north or the south
That's what I call Pizza-Mouth.

If A Grizzly Bear Had Feathers

If a grizzly bear had feathers

And a hummingbird had fur,

We'd hear a big scary TWEET!!

And a cute little grrr!

Caroline

My mother's best friend is Caroline,
They've known each other since they were nine.
Each day they visit or keep in touch,
There never were two people who talk so much.
They talk about kids and jobs and hair
And the people they know and the clothes they wear
And books or movies or what happened today
And they never run out of things to say.
Mom and her best friend, Caroline,
They giggle with each other as if they were nine.
Is that any way for two people to be?
(Well, I guess they're a little like Robin and me.)

Math Problems

I can't *divide* or *multiply*,
A sad and sorry fact,
And, I'm afraid I have to *add*,
I also can't *subtract*.

Mott And Pell

Mr. Mott and Mr. Pell were the very best of friends.
Mott ran Mott's Fine Clothing Store down where Champlain
   Street ends.
So naturally Pell purchased all his clothes from Mr. Mott,
And the two were just as chummy as twin oysters in a pot.

But one day, accidentally, Mott did something mean to Pell.
It was not-on-purpose nasty (what it was I will not tell).
But Pell cried, "I won't wear Mott's clothes one single second
   more!
I will take them off this instant and return them to his store!"

So in a box Pell stuffed his shoes and socks and shirt and tie,
And off he strode toward Champlain Street with fire in his eye.
And furious, he marched to Mott's and cried, "Our friendship's
   gone!"
"Too bad," said Mott, "but do you know you have no clothing
   on?"

Banana Moon

The banana moon is a just-right moon,
Bigger than a fingernail but less than a balloon.
The first stars are here now, so I know it's coming soon,
The just-right, safe-in-bed, sweet banana moon.

What Happens When My Parents Get Ready To Go Out

My mom gets dressed and all made up
And when she's done preparing,
She always asks my father
If he likes the clothes she's wearing.
My dad says, "You look perfect!
You look beautiful! It's great!"
Then, while Mom changes all her clothes,
My dad yells, "Anne, we're late!"

Elevator, Escalator

Elevator, escalator, subway, bus,
Traveling through the city can be a lot of fuss.
It can get a bit confusing for chickens like us,
Elevator, escalator, subway, bus.

Take an elevator up, take an escalator down,
Then a bus through the streets and a subway underground.
Back home on the farm, it's not hard to get around
But the city's complicated when you're going downtown.

Oh, elevator, escalator, subway, bus,
Traveling through the city can be a lot of fuss.
It can get a bit confusing for chickens like us,
Elevator, escalator, subway, bus.

Eleven Reasons My Big Sister Gives For Not Playing With Me When Our Parents Are Out

She stubbed her toe, her back's in pain,
A headache's messing up her brain,
Her throat is sore, her color's pale,
Her stomach hurts, she broke a nail,
Her cough's so bad she thinks she'll die,
She's got a thing-y in her eye,
Her nose is stuffed, her neck is stiff.
But can you guess what happens if
Her boyfriend calls? I say, "Hello? . . .
No, Jane can't talk. She stubbed her toe."
I yell, "Your hero's on the line!"
She grabs the phone . . . "Hi, Paul! . . . I'm fine!!"

Overtired

I am not overtired. I just can't sleep.
I'm lying awake but I won't count sheep.
I am not overtired . . . Did you hear that growl?
I'm sure that it's nothing . . . Did you hear that howl?
Unless it could be . . . Did you hear the floor creak?
Quick, hold your breath and don't dare speak!
Did you hear those scratchy sounds up on the roof?
I know what they are and soon I'll have proof!
Uh-oh, I can feel my heart as it throbs,
There are creatures come to change us into alien blobs!
Oh, no! They turned the light on! . . . Oh, phew! It's just Mom.
"Hi, Mom, we're fine! We're just cool and calm.
We have every single thing that our hearts desired.
Thanks for looking in . . . No, we're not overtired . . ."

Well, I'm sure we're safe but now that Mom's gone
We might as well leave the night-light on
And barricade the door and lock the windows tight.
We'll protect each other, huh? . . . Okay . . . Good night.
. . . The only trouble is they could come without warning
And we'd both be alien blobs in the morning,
So I'd better not sleep . . . But I'm tired . . . And I'm yawning . . .
And . . .
Zzzzzz . . . zzzzzz . . . zzzzzz . . .

(I'm just pretending to be asleep.
That way, if they come, I'll be
ready for them.)

At The Doctor's Office

There are times when I'm brave and times when I'm not,
Guess which one I am as I wait for this shot.
The doctor insists there's no cause for alarm
But that huge needle's not going into *her* arm.
I'll just look away and pray she won't botch it
(You certainly wouldn't expect me to watch it).
I'll get my mind off it, I'll make myself strong,
I'll think of the words to a difficult song,
I'll just dig my fingernails into my hand
To prepare for the torture I know she has planned.
I'm biting my cheek now, I'm holding my breath
As I wait for the end of this fate worse than death.
Uh-oh, she's rubbing on alcohol now,
It can only be seconds until she gives ... "OW!"
"Did that hurt?" says the doctor.
"Hurt? No, of course not."
"You're a pretty brave kid."
"Well, it's only a shot ..."

The First Day Of School

Sarah and I think that the first day of school makes you feel like everyone is staring at you all day long.

It's like they're looking at what you're wearing, and how you comb your hair, and how much you've changed over the summer.

They're listening to the way you talk and checking out whether you're pretty cool or whether you're too full of yourself.

The teachers are looking to see if you're smart or not.

The coaches and gym instructors are looking to see who the good athletes are.

Even the people who work in the cafeteria seem like they're looking to see who eats all their lunch.

Sarah and I think the first day of school is like being onstage all day with a big spotlight on you.

But then comes the second day and everything's back to normal and nobody cares about all that stuff from yesterday and nothing seems like such a big deal anymore.

What Nobody Wants You To Show Them At The Dinner Table

Chewed
Food.

(It's rude.)

Mom And Dad And Bob And Nan

Each of them is proud of having a name
That, forward or backward, is spelled the same.
(Eve likes this poem and so does Anna
And so does Lil and her friend Hannah.)

A Bad Habit

A fingernail biter named Kevin
Tried to quit it at age eighty-seven.
"If I can't learn to clip them,
In poison I'll dip them!"
(Too bad. Now he bites them in heaven.)

President Strickler

I. THINGS CHARLES STRICKLER IS GOOD AT

1) Every subject at school (all A's or A+'s)
2) Sports (the best runner)
3) Seriousness (A+ + +)

II. WHAT HE IS NOT GOOD AT

1) Sense of humor (D–)

III. THINGS CHARLES STRICKLER IS VERY SERIOUS ABOUT

1) What books he will read over the summer
2) What college he will go to eight years from now
3) How he will be a lawyer and get married and have children and go into politics

IV. WHAT WE THINK WILL HAPPEN TO HIM

1) We think he will read a lot of books over the summer
2) We think he will be very successful in college
3) We think he might even get elected President of the U.S. and invite us to the White House to visit him and Mrs. Strickler and Charles Jr.

(We think that if the President invites you to the White House you should probably go, but with President Strickler, we're not sure it would be that much fun.)

My Mom Sings

My mom sings as we walk down the street.
She sings *really loud* as we walk down the street.
When I was very little,
I didn't used to care
But now when Mom starts singing,
I see the people stare.
And now when Mom starts singing,
I wish I weren't there!

(I tried to talk to her about it, but forget it.)

Toothpaste And Igloo

Toothpaste is quite practical
You'll use it most, no doubt,
To paste a tooth back in your mouth
Whenever one falls out.
Igloo is quite similar
For problems small or big—
Just buy a tube of igloo
And glue back your broken ig!

Underwater

Howard once stayed
Underwater for an hour!!
How did he do it?...

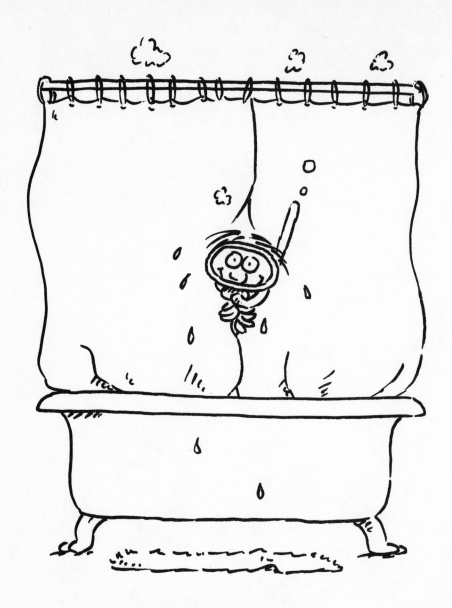

He took a long shower.

A Question About Snow White

If you were Snow White, would you like to live deep in a forest and do nothing all day but

clean house   wash dishes
make beds   mop floors
cook meals   do laundry

for seven people, five of whom were sleepy, sneezy, dopey, bashful, and grumpy all the time?

a) Yes   ☐
b) No   ☐
c) Hmmm . . . ☐

Lost And Found

I lost my dog Beth out in the park.
I lost hold of her leash and she ran with a bark.
I ran after her till I lost my breath,
Then I finally lost sight of my dog Beth.
I lost my patience as I called her name,
So I stopped to play ball and I lost a game.
Then I lost my temper and, sad to say,
As I tried to get home, I lost my way.
Then I lost all hope of seeing Beth again
And I lost control but, suddenly, then . . .
I was cuddling someone furry with doggie-breath,
And I found I'd been dreaming next to my dog Beth.

Wally's Rhyme

The trolley
Took Wally
And Polly,
His collie,
And Molly,
His dolly,
To Follington Square.

And Wally,
So jolly,
With Polly,
His collie,
And Molly,
His dolly,
Met Holly Jones there.

Then Wally
Kissed Holly,
So Polly,
His collie,
And Molly,
His dolly,
Were jolly and gay.

But Wally,
By golly,
Got back on
The trolley
With Polly,
His collie,
And went on his way.

(But Wally left Molly, his dolly,
as a present for Holly and later
they got married and opened
a Mexican food stand called
"Holly's and Wally's Tamales.")

One Special Thing

My friend Anne-Marie probably knows more about dinosaurs than any kid in the world. If some professor needed to know about a dinosaur nobody ever heard of, he could ask Anne-Marie and find out.

With Richard, it's baseball. It's like he's memorized every player's batting average in history. Even people's dads are amazed at how much baseball Richard knows.

And my friend Morgan has a rock collection, a leaf collection, a shell collection, and a bug collection which he will talk about for hours if you let him.

It seems a lot of my friends have one special thing they're crazy about. I don't have a thing like that, but I guess Anne-Marie and Richard and Morgan all need someone who's pretty smart to listen to them and be interested when they talk about their special thing. So I guess that's me and maybe that's my special thing.

The Twelve-Inch Ruler

A wise head of state
Was King Tiny the Great.

Abby's Diary

Dear Diary,
   As you read the following, make checks (√) in the "True" and "False" boxes.

1) **If I liked Kimberly this much** ⬚ **and I found out**

yesterday in school that she only liked me this much ⬚ **, then**

	True	False
a) I would ask her to give me back my purple sweater immediately.	☐	☐
b) I would accidentally-on-purpose tell her that Brian Farnshaw thinks she's gross.	☐	☐
c) I would realize I only liked her this much ⬚ anyway.	☐	☐

2) **If I liked Julia this much** ⬚

and I found out she liked me this much ⬚ **, too, then**

	True	False
a) We would be perfect best friends.	☐	☐
b) We would talk on the phone every day after school.	☐	☐
c) We would start an "I Hate Kimberly" club.	☐	☐

3) If I liked Pam this much ☐☐☐

and I found out that she liked me this much ☐ **, then**

	True	False
a) I'd let her be my friend sometimes.	☐	☐
b) I might put her on my birthday-party list to replace someone whose name begins with K.	☐	☐
c) I'd explain to Pam that if she happened to find a dead mouse and put it in Kimberly's desk, that would be really funny.	☐	☐

True
(If you checked ☑ in every box, you are correct.)

Why It's Hard To Be Romantic
If You're An Octopus

She said, "Put your arms around me, honey,
Won't you hold me tight?"
He said, "By the time I put
   all my arms around you
It'll be next Saturday night."

Jerry

This summer, when the North Road got so hot the tar melted,
Jerry walked on it with bare feet.

I saw him skin his knee once, so bad the blood went down to
his sock and he almost didn't pay attention.

I watched him go off the high diving board for the first time and
he didn't even stop to count to three.

But the night his dog Charley got hit by a car, I saw him from
my window, all alone in his backyard, crying so much he
didn't even hear it when his parents called him.

Homes

If I were a beaver, I'd live in a dam
On a stream that came wandering by.
If I were a turtle, I'd live in a shell
That would keep me all cozy and dry.
If I were an eagle, I'd live in a nest
At the top of a branch overhead.
But since I'm a monster with red shiny eyes and lots of drool . . .
Why, of course, I live under your bed!

If You Make Me Go To Bed Now

If you make me go to bed now
I am sure that I would hear
The sound of a mosquito
Buzzing loudly in my ear.
So, of course, I'd try to swat him
As I saw him try to land,
But I'd miss and break the bed lamp
And I know I'd hurt my hand,
So I'd need to find some bandages
To help to ease the pain,
But, in the dark, I'd bang my knee
So hard I'd need a cane,
And the ache would be so awful
That I wouldn't sleep a wink,
So I'd go to school next morning
And I couldn't even think,
So of course I'd fail my math test
And my other subjects, too,
I'd be so sad and embarrassed
There'd be nothing left to do
Except run away from home
About as far as I could go,
So I'd limp off to Alaska
And I'd trudge through ice and snow,
Till I met a hungry grizzly bear
All fierce and mean and mad
And as that grizzly ate me . . .

I'd remember Mom and Dad.
Yes, I'd think of my dear parents
And their final words to me,
"Get into bed this minute!
Turn that light off instantly!"

Let this poem be a warning
To all parents everywhere:
If you send your kids to bed,
They may be . . .
Digested by a bear.

Danger!

Danger! Don't enter this room!
You'll be risking a perilous doom!
You'll see horror and gore
And my socks on the floor
And a zombie that's fresh from his tomb!

My Parents' Party

I want to stay up for my parents' party
I've *got* to stay up for my parents' party
I *need* to stay up for my parents' party
I don't want to be in bed snoring . . .

. . . They let me stay up for my parents' party
They let me stay up for my parents' party
And now that I'm here at my parents' party . . .
Boy, is it really boring.

Crying

It seems like crying should make you feel worse
But sometimes it happens in just the reverse.
Sometimes you cry about two zillion tears
Till it feels like the tears may come out of your ears.
And then as the bad stuff finds its way out,
You forget what it was you were crying about.

My Brother Has A Clarinet

My brother has a clarinet
That's not like other boys'.
Instead of making music
What my brother makes is noise.
It sounds like parrots squawking
Or a herd of donkeys braying.
Are tires screeching in the street?
No, that's my brother playing.
We run to get our earmuffs on
Before he can begin.
(The only thing that's worse
Is when I play the violin.)

"Will I Let You Borrow My Bike
Because Yours Is Broken? Well,
Do You Think You Could Possibly
Just Stop Teasing Me From Now
Until Monday?"

You don't?
Then I won't.

Deer Friend (A Letter)

 friend,

How are you?

I caught a bad cold out with my Flo.

We were walking with feet in the snow.

My voice got and woe was me,

I had to stay home and miss the spelling

You should have heard me cry and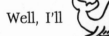

Well, I'll  this letter now and drop it in the mail.

What's  with you? Are you feeling fine?

When you get a chance, please drop me a

Love,
Me

P.S. The animal with horns that's not a deer is a gnu. It goes for lots of walks, so sometimes you have to buy it gnu shoes.

Reading To Me

When I was little, Mom would read to me in bed.
I'd lie under the covers with my eyes closed
And the sound of her voice would make me feel safe and sleepy
  at the same time.
Sometimes, even with the good stories, I'd fall asleep before the
  end.
Now I'm bigger and I can read by myself but still, every once in
  a while, when I'm feeling sad or something,
I'll ask Mom and she'll come in and sit on the edge of the bed
  and touch my head
And read to me again.

Something Green For Dinner

They served something green for dinner
And we wondered what it was.
Kenny whispered that it looked like
Someone's old lawn-mower fuzz.
Dad said, "Try a bite, you'll like it!"
We said, "Tell us, please, what is it?"
Dad said, "Ground up alien fern-tips
From the Martian spaceship's visit."

(They tasted great with the burgers.)

Sharing?

Let me share your bike just once
And here is what I'll do—
All the chores I ever have
I'll gladly share with you!

Millicent's Mother

Millie buttons her coat, gives her mother a kiss,
Then Millicent's mother says something like this:
"Millie, take your umbrella in case there's a storm,
And be sure to wear mittens to keep your hands warm,
And, since it may snow, take your snowshoes and parka,
And pack your big flashlight in case it gets dark-a.
This bicycle pump will help fix a flat tire,
This fire extinguisher puts out a fire,

And take this roast turkey, you may need a snack,
This map and this compass will help you get back,
And take your galoshes, there may be some mud,
And your scuba-dive outfit in case there's a flood,
And in case you get bored, take your toys in your wagon,
And please wear your armor, in case there's a dragon."
"Oh, Mommy!" says Millie. "I don't need all that!"
"Okay," says her mother. "But wear a warm hat."

If I Could Be A . . .

(A Poem Where You Have To Match Things That Have Letters With Things That Have Numbers)

IF

I

COULD

BE

A

1) Ballet Dancer

2) Pet-Store Owner

3) Circus Clown

4) Grocer

5) Teacher

6) Cook in a Chinese Restaurant

7) Magician

8) Veterinarian

JUST

FOR

A

DAY,

I'D

GO

GET

MY

a) sick giraffe

b) wonton soup

c) too-long
   homework
   assignment

d) tutu

e) broccoli

f) little car that 13
   people come
   out of

g) guppies and
   puppies

h) wand that
   makes my
   sister disappear

AND

THEN

WE

COULD

PLAY

Juice, Milk, Water, Soda, Lemonade, Tea

Juice, milk, water, soda, lemonade, tea,
I'm just about as thirsty as a person could be.
I'd appreciate it greatly if you'd please bring me
Some juice, milk, water, soda, lemonade, tea.

Milk, tea, soda, water, lemonade, juice,
I've drunk about as much as a thirsty moose.
If I don't have room for dinner, then my only excuse
Is milk, tea, soda, water, lemonade, juice.

The Family Next Door

Their father is very best friends with our dad,
Their mom is great pals with our mother.
Their sisters hang out with Melinda and Kate
And even the dogs like each other.
Their whole family matches up perfect with ours
Except that they don't have a brother.
(And that's why I couldn't care less if they move
To some distant planet or other.)

I've Got A Lot Of Homework

I've got a lot of homework
But I'm tired and it's late.
Doing homework when I'm tired
Makes the homework not so great.
I could do it in the morning
But then I'd be late for school.
So . . .
I just won't do my homework.
(Phew! I'm glad that I'm so cool!)

(Just kidding, Mom and Dad.)

Rocks And Balls

Thousands and thousands of years ago, before the first ball was
   invented, cave people had rocks to play with.
They'd take a big rock and toss it through a hoop and play
   basketrock.
When they wanted to hit something back and forth across a net,
   they'd use a tennis rock.
They'd also have great fun kicking around a footrock, which is
   why many cave people had sore feet.
Families would go to the rockpark to watch their favorite teams
   play baserock, and, in the seventh inning, everyone would
   stand up and sing "Take Me Out to the Rockgame."
Everyone loved playing games with all kinds of rocks.
Then, one summer, some kids were tossing
      around a big, brightly colored beach rock when suddenly
      somebody had an idea
      and invented the ball.
Well, things changed immediately.
Now, suddenly, a basketrock became
      a basket*ball* and bouncing
      was invented.
Now tennis players could hit the
      ball back without breaking their
      racquets and dodgeball became
      much less painful.
Well, of course, very soon no one
      used rocks in games anymore
      because the ball was such
      a great invention.
And everybody was very happy,
      except the people who sold rocks.
But that's progress.

In The Dark

The night I slept over at Laurie's,
We started talking in the dark.
We talked for a very long time about everything—
About our parents, and the kids at school,
What we'd be like when we grew up
Or what we'd do if we met a rock star.
Sometimes what we said was serious
And sometimes we giggled so loud we had to bite our pillows.
Every once in a while, we'd even say good-night.
But then, after a minute, one of us would start talking again.
We just kept talking until, finally, we were so tired that when we
    said good-night,
We knew this time it was for real.
Except after a minute, I said to Laurie that I wished we were
    sisters so we could talk like this all the time.
But Laurie said no, she had a sister and they didn't talk like we
    were talking.
Laurie said probably only friends could talk the way we did.
Then we were quiet for a minute. And then we both said good-
    night one last time.

Copying Machine

I'd like to put my brother through a copying machine.
I'd make a real-life copy of him being cruel and mean.
Then next time he was bad, I'd take the copy off the shelf
'Cause I'd love to see my brother being nasty to himself.

Waiting For Louie

I'm waiting here for Louie
Because Louie's always late.
When you make a date with Louie
It's just wait and wait and wait.
So have you got a toothbrush
And pajamas I could borrow?
(By the time that Louie gets here,
It may be sometime tomorrow.)

Your Nose Is Running

"Your nose is running," Mother said.
I answered, "Wow! That's really neat!"
"Why's that?" she asked. I said, "Because
I never knew my nose had feet."

The Last Day Of School

I'm so glad it's finally over!
I've waited all year for this day!
It's ended, concluded and finished!
The one word for that is *hooray*!
So why am I getting this feeling
That maybe I'll miss everyone?
And why is there always some sadness
When everything's over and done?

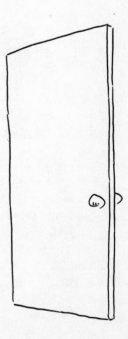

Index

To Deb Futter who, in addition to everything else, made it all a good time; to Annie Boylan whose spirit and good sense were taken full advantage of throughout; and to Rob Weisbach who was the glue; thanks and more thanks for their help in the making of this book.

J.M.

JEFF MOSS was one of the original creators of *Sesame Street*. Serving as head writer and composer-lyricist, he has won twelve Emmys and written the songs for four Grammy-winning records. Moss's music and lyrics for *The Muppets Take Manhattan* earned him an Academy Award nomination. His first book of poetry was *The Butterfly Jar* and he has authored and coauthored more than a dozen books under the *Sesame Street* name. Moss created the personalities of some of television's most memorable characters, including Oscar the Grouch and the Cookie Monster. His hit songs include "Rubber Duckie," "I Love Trash," "The People in Your Neighborhood," and "I Don't Want to Live on the Moon."

CHRIS DEMAREST is the author and illustrator of *The Lunatic Adventure of Kitman and Willy*, *Kitman and Willy at Sea*, *No Peas for Nellie*, and *Morton and Sidney*, and he illustrated Jeff Moss's poems in *The Butterfly Jar*. He lives in Connecticut.